Beautiful As You Are

Introduction

The world is a beautiful place. There are many wonderful children from different places and various cultures that make this world interesting to us all.

All the children in various parts of the world have different colours: brown, black, white and they all have different hair colours: red, white, brown and black.

Sadly some people use our differences as a reason to hate one another instead of seeing it as what makes us beautiful together. Everyone is different and unique in their own way.

You are also important to this world. You are part of the many people that make the world special.

Do you want to find out why you should love yourself? Do you know why each person from each race, color and language is unique?

What is the best way to face a challenge?

How can the world become a better place? What can you do to make your life and that of others awesome?

Read this book to answer the questions then you can sing your beautiful song.

You will be glad you did!

Have you ever sung a fun little song?

A song about how everyone can get along?

People who are red, brown, yellow, black, or white?

They all deserve to shine brightly in the night.

When we are together, we will become strong.

We can face any challenge, no matter how long.

Together we become a community complete.

One that is ready to continually compete.

Except songs that are sung are not lives that all live.

Instead of together, many find faults or refuse to forgive.

And when nothing can be found, differences becomes an excuse.

To offer mean words or provide some other abuse.

Each person has their own unique look.

One that helps them find their own little nook.

Where they can be whomever they want to be.

Offering their talents for the whole world to see.

Each person has their own personality.

Their approach to life provides us all with clarity.

It may be a laugh. It could be a good cry.

Or the courage to always be willing to ask "Why?"

Why do some focus on melanin instead of ideas so great?

Why do some allow negativity to fester into hate?

Why can we sing songs as kids about how we can all get along?

But then allow race to control who can or cannot belong?

The answer is simple, but its meaning is tough.

And the results of the answer can be a little rough.

Because hatred offered outward comes from a hatred within.

Those who don't celebrate differences aren't comfortable in their own skin.

In order to love others, we must also be able to love our own heart.

We must embrace ourselves and allow joy to never, not ever depart.

For if we look for bad things, that's what the world will bring.

No matter what the lyrics may be in the songs that we sing.

We must let our lights shine bright for everyone to see.

And we must accept what our light means in the definition of "me."

Then we must embrace others, even if they are trapped in the night.

Because everyone has something beautiful that can become the brightest light.

So let us allow our reflections
to reflect the rest of the world.

Encourage every race, culture,
and color to have their talents unfurled.

Block the hate before it rises so
there are no more excusing surprises.

And the songs of our youth will
reflect tomorrow's richest prizes.

Conclusion

Every child is special. You are special and so are all the other children around you. Your difference is what makes you special.

It is what makes you unique and beautiful. It is the reason why you should love yourself.

When you love yourself from your heart, there will be no reason to spread hate. No one is better than another.

Even though we have different views because of our cultures, race and diverse background, we are all beautiful together.

Don't look down at others from different race, culture and color. See them as the reason why life is beautiful.

Embrace yourself wholly from your heart; embrace others too, then the world will become a better place.

Made in the USA
San Bernardino, CA
14 April 2018